THE CREATIVE CURRICULUM®
LearningGames®

48–60 Months

Joseph Sparling and Isabelle Lewis

Foreword by Diane Trister Dodge

Teaching Strategies Inc.
Washington, DC

This book of *LearningGames* is being shared with the family of

_____

Editor: Kai-leé Berke
Design: Carla Uriona
Layout/production: Tony MacFarlane and Abner Nieves

Published by:
Teaching Strategies, Inc.
P.O. Box 42243
Washington, DC 20015
www.TeachingStrategies.com

ISBN: 978-1-933021-62-1

Printed and bound in the United States of America

2012	2011	2010	2009	2008	2007
6	5	4	3	2	1

Contents

T226g
ec: mt
vol. 5

THE CREATIVE CURRICULUM®
LearningGames®

Foreword

Dear Parents,

It gives me great pleasure to introduce you to an exciting program called *The Creative Curriculum® LearningGames®*. The games are designed to build the kinds of skills that lead to successful, lifelong learning for your child. You are the key to making this happen.

On a regular basis you will be receiving a colorful handout describing simple and fun games to play with your child. They don't require any special toys or materials. You can do them as part of your everyday experiences with your child. But they can make a big difference, and they already have made a difference for thousands of children and families.

There are five different sets of *LearningGames* for children of different ages. You will receive only the games appropriate for your child. It's never too soon to start. Right from birth, your child is learning and growing. The experiences you provide during the first 5 years of life will help to build your child's brain, develop thinking skills, promote social skills, and build your child's confidence as a learner.

You are your child's first and most important teacher. Everything you do with your child, everything you say, every song you sing, and every object you give your child to play with teach important lessons. One of the wonderful results of using these games is that they help you to build a positive relationship with your child. And as your child is learning, you are as well. You will gain an understanding of child development and many practical ideas for guiding your child's learning.

Many programs using the *LearningGames* are also implementing either *The Creative Curriculum® for Infants, Toddlers & Twos* or *The Creative Curriculum® for Preschool*. As the lead author on these comprehensive curriculum materials, I am very excited to be able to offer this parent component, too. Children benefit the most when the important adults in their lives—their parents, caregivers, teachers, health care specialists, or home visitors—are working together to support their learning and growth.

I wish you great enjoyment and success,

Diane Trister Dodge
President
Teaching Strategies, Inc.

Acknowledgments

Many people helped in the preparation of *The Creative Curriculum®* *LearningGames®*. We would like to thank Kai-leé Berke and Heather Baker for their thoughtful writing contributions and for finding wonderful children's books that enhance each game. Thank you to Nancy Guadagno, Sharon Samber, Toni Bickart, and Rachel Tickner, our editors, for their attention to detail. We appreciate the work of Carla Uriona, who designed the new format for the activities, and Abner Nieves and Tony MacFarlane for their careful layout work. Thanks to Nancy Guadagno and Kai-leé Berke for their patience and persistence in moving the writing, editing, and production process forward.

Checklist for
The Creative Curriculum® LearningGames®: 48-60 months

I have shared the LearningGames *checked below with the family of* _____

Given to Family	LearningGames Activity Number and Title	Date Given to Family/Notes
☐	151. Sharing Likes and Dislikes	
☐	152. My Family	
☐	153. Retelling the Story	
☐	154. Inspect and Collect	
☐	155. Bigger Than Me	
☐	156. How About You?	
☐	157. Fork Foods	
☐	158. Syllable Jump	
☐	159. When, How, Why?	
☐	160. Move Up Five	
☐	161. To and From	
☐	162. My Favorite Things	
☐	163. Search in Pairs	
☐	164. Serious Questions	
☐	165. A Calendar of Special Memories	
☐	166. Our Story	

THE CREATIVE CURRICULUM®
LearningGames®

Given to Family	*LearningGames* Activity Number and Title	Date Given to Family/Notes
☐	167. First, Next, Last	
☐	168. Build a Person	
☐	169. I Wonder How She's Feeling	
☐	170. This Is Who I Am	
☐	171. Add to the Tale	
☐	172. Sort Any Way You Like	
☐	173. Scrambled Stories	
☐	174. Which Is Best?	
☐	175. Little by Little	
☐	176. Show Me How It Feels	
☐	177. Today I Can	
☐	178. I'll Get It Myself	
☐	179. Mailing a Letter	
☐	180. Double Treasure	
☐	181. How Do You Walk When…?	
☐	182. Cut New Lines	
☐	183. Three-Corner Catch	
☐	184. I'd Like Help	
☐	185. My History in Clothes	
☐	186. Rules to Grow On	

Given to Family	LearningGames Activity Number and Title	Date Given to Family/Notes
☐	187. Tell How	
☐	188. Color and Number Cards	
☐	189. Let's Imagine	
☐	190. Wondering What Caused It	
☐	191. Clothes for Tomorrow	
☐	192. We Play Relay	
☐	193. Let's Celebrate	
☐	194. Rhyming	
☐	195. Counting Higher	
☐	196. Think It Through	
☐	197. Silly Simon	
☐	198. Tricky Directions	
☐	199. Same Sounds	
☐	200. Noticing Words	

What Your Child May Be Doing
Four-Year-Olds (48–60 months)

Social/Emotional Development

Can follow simple instructions and sustain attention

Can learn to solve problems through negotiation and compromise

Have strong emotions and are learning to name and express them appropriately

Develop friendships and may have a best friend

Are learning to play games with rules

Cognitive Development

Talk about what they are doing and explain their ideas

Represent what they learned through drawings, constructions, and dramatic play

Ask many questions: What? Why? How?

Make connections between new experiences and ideas and what they already know

Understand concepts related to number, size, weight, color, textures, distance, position, and time

Follow two- to three-step directions

Physical Development

Demonstrate basic gross motor skills (for example, running, jumping, hopping, galloping)

Pedal, steer, and turn corners on a tricycle or other wheeled vehicle

Show balance while moving

Climb up and down stairs easily

Demonstrate throwing, kicking, and catching skills

Use tools for writing and drawing (for example, drawing objects and shapes, writing letters and words)

Fasten clothing

Build detailed structures with smaller materials

Use tools, such as scissors, successfully

Complete interlocking puzzles

Language and Literacy Development

Retell familiar stories, mastering the correct sequencing of events

Learn most of the rules of grammar without direct instruction

Understand that printed words convey messages

Memorize songs, rhymes, and books with repetitive language patterns

Learn time concepts; talk about yesterday and tomorrow

Learn print concepts, such as that English text is written and read from left to right

Sharing Likes and Dislikes

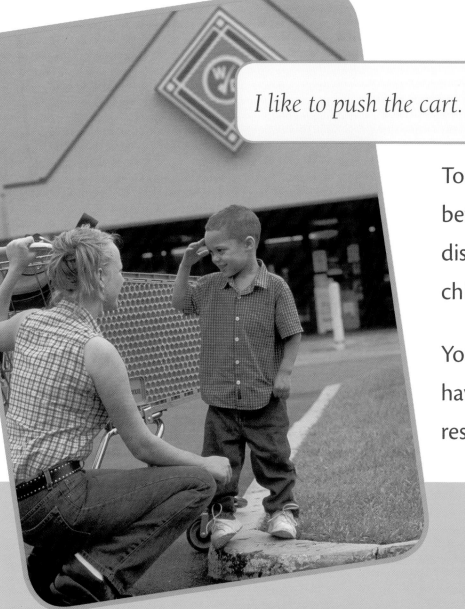

I like to push the cart.

To get to know each other better, express your likes and dislikes and encourage your child to do the same.

Your child will learn that people have many opinions and his are respected and valued.

Why this is important

When we do not like something or someone, words are a useful substitute for physical aggression. When you model a way to express what your child likes or dislikes about a situation, he will learn that feelings have names and can be talked about. Being able to express his feelings is important as your child develops a strong sense of self and builds relationships with others.

What you do

- Talk about a situation, such as going to the doctor, with your child: *I like going to the doctor. There are nice magazines in the waiting room, and the doctor helps us feel better. What do you like about going to the doctor?*

- Give your child time to think. Accept his opinion when he answers.

- Add to the conversation by talking about what you do not like about going to the doctor. *I don't like going to the doctor because sometimes we have to wait. What do you not like about going to the doctor?*

- Accept his feelings and comment calmly. *So that's what you don't like.*

- Be sure to make your child feel comfortable with his answers. Trying to change his feelings or making him feel guilty about them will discourage him from expressing them again.

- Refrain from correcting misinformation during this activity. Listen, and help him put his feelings into words.

Another idea

Many topics work for this activity such as going to the supermarket, birthday parties, big sisters, long car rides, etc. Always give your full attention to your child during the conversation.

Let's read together!

I Like Myself
by Karen Beaumont

My Family

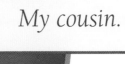

My cousin.

With your child, make and talk about a display of family pictures organized into groups.

Your child will gain understanding and words to help him talk about family relationships.

Why this is important

Your child will enjoy seeing and talking about the pictures of his family and will begin to associate each with the real person. At an age when children try to understand concepts by sorting them into groups and categories, it is helpful for them to gain some knowledge of the relationships among family members. Words like *aunt* and *uncle* will gain more meaning for your child as he begins to understand that one person can be many things (*old, young, sister, mother, aunt*) and fit into more than one category.

What you do

- Put two pieces of poster board or construction paper on the wall within your child's reach.

- Label one poster "Mommy's Family" and the other "Daddy's Family," or use other titles as needed to represent two sides of your child's family.

- Put a photo of each parent next to the label and invite your child to put a picture of himself on each poster.

- Encourage family members to send photos to be added to the posters. When your child receives a photo, explain the family relationship before adding it to the correct poster: *Aunt Marie is Daddy's little sister. Grandpapa was their Daddy.*

- Give explanations using words *brother, sister, uncle,* etc.

- Point out a relative's place in the family before a visit: *Uncle John is Grandmother's son and Mommy's brother.*

Another idea

If your family is small or you and your child are not in contact with all parts of the family, make one of the posters a "Love Family" consisting of the friends who play the roles of aunts, uncles, cousings, and grandparents for him.

Let's read together!

No Mirrors in My Nana's House
by Ysaye M. Barnwell

Retelling the Story

And they felt scared.

And they were afraid.

Share a short, original story with your child that she can retell to a puppet or a friend.

This gives your child practice in recalling the main points of a story and prepares her to remember main ideas later when she learns to read.

Why this is important

Storytelling gives your child an opportunity to remember and retell main events. Although the details of the story may change, she can piece together the main points of the story. Becoming familiar with stories and how they work will help your child when she begins to read.

What you do

- Find a puppet or stuffed animal that your child likes. Explain to her that you can tell her a story that she can share with the puppet: *You could tell Charlie a story. I'll tell you a brand new one he's never heard. Listen carefully so later you'll be able to tell the story to him.*

- Begin your story with a description of the main character, such as raccoon, followed by three clear events. Add as many details as you think your child can remember. For example:

    First, he went looking for someone to play with.

    Then, he met a scary bear who chased him home.

    At last, inside his own house he found his rabbit friend who had come to play.

- Encourage your child to retell the story to the puppet or stuffed animal.

- Make the puppet or stuffed animal an enthusiastic listener so that your child stays engaged in the storytelling.

Ready to move on?

Invite the puppet to retell a story to your child, but make sure to change a few details so that the puppet makes some mistakes. This gives your child an opportunity to correct the puppet and recall more about the story.

Let's read together!

The Hello, Goodbye Window
by Norton Juster

Inspect and Collect

I found a bumpy rock!

Over several weeks, encourage your child to find treasures, display them, and talk about them.

Your child will express his personal choices and begin to maintain an interest in things over a period of time.

THE
CREATIVE CURRICULUM®
LearningGames®
Copyright 2007 Joseph Sparling

Why this is important

You can encourage your child to notice interesting objects in his environment and then help him sustain that interest by keeping the found items available as a collection. He will have the chance to make choices, develop his own personal tastes, and maintain a project for a period of time.

What you do

- Notice when your child picks up and admires small objects he finds. Begin by talking about his new discovery: *I see that rock has gray and white specks in it. It'd be fun to save it. I wonder if there are any other interesting rocks around here.*

- Discuss how the gathered items could be saved as a collection. Your child can create a display of his new treasures.

- Try displaying hard items like rocks and shells in a jar of water to make the colors brighter. Place fragile items in the individual sections of an egg carton. Stick feathers in a small foam block.

- Talk with your child about other ways his collection can be displayed.

- Admire the collection often and wonder aloud about other items that could be added to it.

Another idea

Allow your child to dismantle his collection at any time. He may find interest in a new group of objects.

Let's read together!

Flotsam
by David Wiesner

Bigger Than Me

> This box is bigger than Jim.

Invite your child to compare his body to other objects (such as a box) or spaces (such as a room).

Your child will begin to understand that size is relative and he may use phrases such as *smaller than*.

> Tell me about the box James has his foot in.

Why this is important

Your child will understand *bigger than* and *smaller than* if he can look at an object and compare it to something else. Making these comparisons gives him greater experience in using size words, and he learns to relate one object to another to judge size. Learning to consider an object in relation to another object is a basic step in evaluating and comparing.

What you do

- Stand with your child in the middle of a room. Say, *Without moving from our spot, let's try to touch the walls. Now the ceiling!*

- Point out why you were unsuccessful: *The room is big. It is bigger than we are.*

- Go with him into a closet or smaller room and repeat the action. Point out, *This room is smaller than the other.*

- Listen carefully to his comments to make sure he understands *bigger* and *smaller*.

- Offer him two cardboard boxes. One box should be big enough for him to sit inside, the other should be too small for him to get into.

- Suggest he get in the smaller one. Ask him why he thinks he does not fit. Help him use the words *smaller than I am.*

- Invite him to try to sit in the big box. Hand him the small box so that he can compare the two boxes up close.

Another idea

Make a large rope circle on the floor and invite your child to march around it. Then form a smaller circle for comparison. He can also use his body to measure by comparing objects to his hand, thumbnail, or foot. Let him find something that is *smaller than my thumbnail.*

Let's read together!

The Dinosaur Who Lived in My Backyard
by B.G. Hennessy

How About You?

Who has a cat at home?

Me! I do!

Use a puppet to talk and ask questions that encourage your child to talk about herself.

Through this conversation your child will express and expand her own concept of herself.

THE **CREATIVE CURRICULUM**® **LearningGames**®
Copyright 2007 Joseph Sparling

Why this is important

A puppet can help your child express her own concept of herself. Even if she answers only in single syllables or nods, this game gives her a chance to think and talk about herself. As your child answers questions about herself, she is slowly forming her present and future self-image. She will be encouraged to expand her vocabulary by copying and using words she hears others say.

What you do

- Choose a puppet to share with your child. Invite her to join the puppet in a conversation.

- Form simple questions, spoken by the puppet, for your child to answer. A few sample questions could be:

Puppet:	**Child:**
Hi, *my name is Calvin. What's your name?*	*Ann.*
Oh, Ann is a pretty name! I'm 2, how old are you?	*Four.*
That sounds so big! I can't wait until I'm 4. Do you like cats?	*Yes.*
Me, too. They're so soft. Do you know anyone with a cat?	*I have one.*
Oh, you are lucky! Do you help feed your cat?	*Sometimes.*
I bet your Mommy is glad to have you as a helper.	*Yes.*
What is your favorite thing about your cat?	*She sits in my lap and she purrs.*

- Encourage your child to use words that the puppet has used. For example, if the puppet says *fuzzy*, ask a question such as: *How does your cat's fur feel?* This will prompt your child to remember and use the new word.

Another idea

Return to the puppet activity whenever your child may have something new to share, such as a new pair of shoes or details about a visiting relative.

Let's read together!

Little Bunny Finger Puppet Book
  by Klaartje van der Put

Fork Foods

Are green beans a fork food?

Ask your child about specific foods at meal times and help her determine whether or not each food is eaten with a fork, a spoon, or fingers.

This experience will encourage her to classify things in a new way: how they are eaten.

Why this is important

By talking about foods and how they are eaten at mealtime, your child will learn the names of foods and begin to classify them. She will begin to think about the different ways a food can be eaten. A strawberry, for example, can be eaten using her fingers or with a fork. Working with food and the appropriate eating utensils is part of handling the ritual of eating in culturally acceptable ways.

What you do

● Invite your child to make three charts with you. The charts should be labeled "Fork Foods," "Spoon Foods," and "Finger Foods." Your child can add to the charts by drawing a fork, spoon, or hand under the related heading.

● Place the charts in a prominent part of the kitchen. Go to the chart before each meal and talk about what food you will serve: *Tonight I cooked fish and rice. We are also having applesauce. What will you use to eat the fish: a fork, a spoon, or your fingers?*

● Offer your child a pencil or crayon to draw a picture of the food on the appropriate chart. If you are eating something that comes in a package such as frozen vegetables or cereal, invite your child to cut out the label and tape it to the correct chart. Repeat the process with each food in the meal.

● Encourage your child to think about which foods might belong on more than one chart, such as the rice.

● Return to the chart regularly with your child as she thinks of more foods to add.

Another idea

You can play a version of the game when you go to the supermarket. Walk through the produce department and look together for a fork food, a spoon food, and a finger food to take home. Talking about foods in the produce section encourages your child's interest in trying healthy fruits and vegetables.

Let's read together!

Eating the Alphabet: Fruits & Vegetables from A to Z
by Lois Ehlert

Syllable Jump

Ma–ri–a.

Maria.

Show your child how to take steps or jump to match the syllables of her own name.

She will increase her awareness of the parts that make up words.

THE
CREATIVE CURRICULUM®
LearningGames®
Copyright 2007 Joseph Sparling

Why this is important

The actions of your child's own body can help her pay attention to the sounds of words and parts of words. When a young child learns something through her body as well as her mind she understands it better. Hearing and responding to the smaller sound units in words (syllables) is part of the foundation for reading and spelling.

What you do

- Write your child's name on a piece of construction paper, allowing plenty of cutting space between each syllable. (If all of your child's names are one syllable, use the name of a favorite person, pet or stuffed animal.)

- Help your child cut the syllables apart. Touch the syllables as you say them. *Kim-ber-ly. Grand-pa.*

- On the floor, ground, or sidewalk, invite your child to help you make a row of connected boxes—like a small hopscotch drawing, going from right to left. The boxes can be made outside with sidewalk chalk or inside with masking tape. There should be one box for each syllable in the child's name.

- Help your child put the cut-apart syllables in the boxes going from left to right.

- Explain that you are going to jump into one box for each syllable of her name. As you slowly repeat her name, hop into a box for each syllable. A bunny hop (jumping with both feet) works well in this game.

- Invite your child to try. Hold her hand for balance if she needs it.

Another idea

If your child is ready and interested, let her jump on the syllables of some other words, such as her last name, the name of her preschool, or her favorite food.

Let's read together!

Chicka Chicka Boom Boom
by Bill Martin Jr and John Archambault

When, How, Why?

Why is it so cold?

In daily events or after reading a book, occasionally ask a question that begins with one of the words *when, how,* or *why.*

These questions will stimulate your child to think more deeply about time, processes, and reasons.

Why this is important

Asking *when, how,* or *why* questions will deepen the level of your child's thinking. To answer them she will need to talk about time, process, and reasons. This encourages her to give longer answers with several parts. Thinking about *how* and *why* are some of the hardest tasks we do throughout life. This early practice can give your child a pattern of successful thinking to follow and to build on as she grows older. When she answers questions during book reading, she is building her early literacy skills.

What you do

● Ask your child *when, how,* and *why* questions during conversation or reading. *When do we eat breakfast? How did you dig that deep hole? Why did the three bears go for a walk?*

● Give your child plenty of time to think about her answers to these challenging questions. Return to simpler questions if she struggles to answer.

● Pause after reading a page of a book together and ask one of the questions, so she can think about the story.

Another idea

Continue to ask questions that gently test your child's knowledge. Many everyday moments such as riding in the car, taking a bath, or drawing with chalk can offer opportunities for question-and-answer sessions with your child.

Let's read together!

Red Leaf, Yellow Leaf
by Lois Ehlert

Move Up Five

One, two, three, four, five.

Create an easy board game that lets your child move a marker as he counts from one to five.

Your child will remember and understand these basic numbers if he has a lot of enjoyable practice using them.

THE
CREATIVE CURRICULUM®
LearningGames®
Copyright 2007 Joseph Sparling

Why this is important

Your child may already know how to count to five, but he may not understand that each number from one to five stands for a definite quantity. He will practice using the words for numbers up to five as he verbally and physically counts out five spaces on the game board. Numbers are used every day by your child, and he will continue to practice counting skills as he grows older.

What you do

- Make five cards that either have one, two, three, four, or five dots on them. Make the dots large enough for your child to point to and count them.

- Find or make a simple path game board with spaces large enough for a game marker to touch each square as your child advances the piece.

- Invite your child to join you in a counting game. Using your path game board and cards with dots to determine the count, the two of you will take turns moving your markers. Explain the game to him: *We'll take turns choosing a card. The dots on the card will tell us how many spaces to move our marker.*

- Practice choosing a card and counting the dots.

- Encourage your child to move the marker in a hopping motion as you play so that each space can be counted as it is touched.

- Emphasize differences in numbers by saying: *Five! That's a lot.* Or, *Two is a quick hop.*

- Stop the game when your child's interest ends, which may be before the game is over.

Another idea

Throughout your day together, invite your child to count out five objects when he sees them.

Let's read together!

Rooster's Off to See the World
by Eric Carle

To and From

Can you run to the big tire?

Suggest that your child move to and from a variety of locations. Your child will get some exercise, and his direct, active experience will lead to a deeper understanding of position words.

Why this is important

Talking about *to* and *from* increases your child's understanding of these basic directional words and helps him learn how to use them. Little words like *to* and *from* show specific relationships between actions and objects. In this activity, you are giving names to his actions. *To the table* conveys a different idea than *from the table* or *on the table*.

What you do

- Name your child's actions as he plays. Talk about what he is doing (*running*) and in what direction (*from* or *to the big tire*).

- Invite him to repeat the action, but change the direction. For example:

    You're running to the tree. Can you run to the fence? It's farther.

    You're skipping from the swings to the sandbox. Can you skip from the sandbox to the slide? It's uphill.

- Add labels such as *uphill* or *farther* to introduce new descriptive concepts.

- Invite him to suggest an action to you. Talk about the action as you carry out his directions.

Ready to move on?

Increase the number of prepositions used in this activity. Try words such as *behind, between, beside,* etc. Sometimes ask, *Where are you going?* Listen for his answers to include the new words he has learned.

Let's read together!

Muncha! Muncha! Muncha!
    by Candace Fleming

My Favorite Things

These are my favorite instruments!

Help your child become aware of her favorite things by asking questions that prompt her to think about her own opinions.

Your child will learn that her ideas tell information about herself and are interesting to other people.

THE
CREATIVE CURRICULUM®
LearningGames®

Why this is important

By supporting your child's personal choices, you send her the message that her choices are of interest to you and you respect her opinions. Though her tastes may change, the good feelings she gets from having them respected stays with her. This helps her to feel good about herself and to continue to make thoughtful personal choices.

What you do

- Invite your child to play a word game with you.

- Make a statement about her favorite things, but leave out the last word for her to complete.

- Use her name in each statement to give her a stronger sense of how important her own tastes are. For example:

  Jennie's favorite person is _____.

  Jennie's favorite hat is _____.

  Jennie's favorite story is _____.

  Jennie's favorite food is_____.

- Affirm each statement without making a judgment about her choice: *Oh, green is your favorite color. Is that why you are wearing a green shirt?*

Another idea

Sometimes play this game by inviting her to gather some of her favorite items together. Encourage her to talk about each one. Remember that her tastes may change each time you play the game.

Let's read together!

If the Dinosaurs Came Back
by Bernard Most

Search in Pairs

I found it!

Invite your child and a playmate (a pair) to search for objects such as a brush and a comb (another pair).

The children will start to understand that things and people sometimes need a partner to do a complete job.

Why this is important

Your child will learn that partners work together well if they each do their own special part of the whole task. By playing this game several times, he may begin to notice objects in the world that function in pairs. Awareness of partnerships helps him begin to understand that people and things are often interdependent.

What you do

● Introduce a game to your child and one of his friends by naming an object, such as a key. Then ask, *What goes with a key? What does a key need in order to work?*

● Prompt them with as many questions as necessary to help them determine the answer: *Where do we put the key to turn it?*

● Take them to the door when they answer *door* or *lock*. Invite them to use the key in the keyhole.

● Explain to the children that they are a pair, too, who will be working together.

● Invite them to help you think of a pair of objects, such as a toothbrush and toothpaste. Together, decide who will be responsible for finding each part of the pair.

● Tell the children, *Bring it back here. Or, Think of a way to show it to me.*

● Talk about each object the children bring and how the objects need each other to function.

● Point out how the children worked together to find the objects that go together.

Another idea

A few other pairs that work well are light and switch, brush and comb, soap and water, shoe and sock, and paper and pencil.

Let's read together!

Two Little Trains
by Margaret Wise Brown

Serious Questions

Why did our turtle die?

Give simple but thoughtful answers to your child's *how* and *why* questions.

From your honest answers to serious questions, your child will begin to build his own viewpoint and values.

THE CREATIVE CURRICULUM®
LearningGames®

Why this is important

Answering your child's serious questions with brief, honest replies helps your child build knowledge and learn your values. Asking questions is a way for your child to get information on facts and attitudes. Children build their value system on the answers others give them, how those answers are given, and their own experiences.

What you do

- Give your child serious answers to questions as they naturally come up during your day together.

- Keep your answers brief and sincere. A detailed, scientific explanation is often not needed.

- Remember that your child will ask for more information if interested. Even questions about topics such as sex, death, or divorce can be answered very simply.

- Assume that when your child asks a question such as *Why did our turtle die?* he is also asking the implied question, *What do you feel about pets and death?*

- Consider this activity as a way to pass on your important values and attitudes.

- Share answers with your child as often as necessary to make him feel at ease with the subject.

Another idea

You may notice your child's anxiety about a topic before he has asked a question. Feel free to approach him and welcome any questions he has. Remind him that you are always available to talk with him openly about serious subjects.

Let's read together!

Two Homes
by Claire Masurel

A Calendar of Special Memories

You're putting the movie ticket on the calendar.

Help your child put pictures and words on a calendar to remind her of recent events.

The calendar will act as a memory aid, helping your child extend her ability to remember.

THE
CREATIVE CURRICULUM®
LearningGames®
Copyright 2007 Joseph Sparling

Why this is important

A calendar can include pictures and words that will help your child recall an event and tell about it. Putting written words under pictures stimulates her interest in print and literacy. Using words to express her memories can give your child the pleasure of sharing her memories and ideas. Memory is necessary for all learning. Using records to jog the memory is an effective tool.

What you do

- Find or make a calendar with day spaces large enough to contain a small picture.

- Record special events with your child by inviting her to paste or draw a picture of the event on the calendar.

- Talk with her about the event as you mark it on the calendar: *Here is a little picture of shoes like your new ones. Let's cut it out and stick it on your calendar. That will help you remember the day we bought them.*

- Look at the calendar with her a few hours later. Ask her to recall what the picture represents.

- Invite her to share these events with family members and friends. Limit the number of events marked. Choose events to remember based on what your child considers significant.

- Review all the pictures each time a new one is added to the calendar. Keep tape, glue, and magazines nearby so that your child can readily look for pictures as needed.

Another idea

Slowly remove yourself from the choosing process. Allow your child to completely decide what to include on the calendar. She may surprise you with events she remembers.

Let's read together!

Diary of a Wombat
by Jackie French

Our Story

Tell a story to your child, pausing at several points to let him add some parts.

Your child's creativity will blossom as he thinks of new ideas and tries them out in storytelling.

The eagle said, we can...

...fly over the mountain.

Why this is important

Creative storytelling provides a safe opportunity for your child to try out new ideas. When he adds ideas, he can use his imagination to change the outcome of the story. Telling a story is good preparation for the later task of creative writing.

What you do

- Invite your child to join you in telling a story. For the first few times, you may need to tell the majority of the story, only pausing occasionally to encourage him to add a word or sentence.

- Begin a story with simple details such as: *Once upon a time, a little rabbit was hopping down the forest path. He looked up in an oak tree, and he saw...*

- Pause for your child's idea, then continue with the details he provides: *Down came the squirrel and said, "Let's go to the...."* Continue the story this way.

- Tell short stories until he feels comfortable and confident with this storytelling format.

- Wait for him to offer more information about the characters and plot. He may provide more than just a one-or two-word answer after several practice stories. Prompt him by asking, *Did anything else happen?*

Another idea

Use this game with your child and other family members or friends by letting them take turns adding to the story.

Let's read together!

Tuesday
by David Wiesner

First, Next, Last

First we find the things we need.

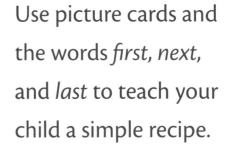

Use picture cards and the words *first*, *next*, and *last* to teach your child a simple recipe.

You child's ability to remember the order of events in a process will improve.

Yes!

THE CREATIVE CURRICULUM® LearningGames®

Copyright 2007 Joseph Sparling

Why this is important

This game provides a fun situation for learning sequencing. Your child will see that some events happen in a given order. Following a recipe builds skills that will help him remember the order of events. Many tasks such as telling a story, bathing, dressing, or riding a bicycle must be done in a particular order to be successful.

What you do

- Invite your child to help you make something from a simple recipe.

- Show him three index cards, and explain that as you work you will draw pictures of what you did.

- Pick up one card and say, *This card is for what we do first. First, we collect the things we need.* As you name the objects (*bowl, spoon, measuring cup*, and *water*), make a simple outline drawing of each object on the card.

- Collect the items together, and review: *First, we found the things we needed.*

- Explain the next step and ask for his help. *Next, we have to put the JELL-O® and the hot water together. How could we do that?* Wait for his suggestion and respond: *Right, we put them in the bowl and mix them. That's the next step. Let me put that on the card.*

- Review the completed step, and then move on to the last step: *The last thing we do is put the JELL-O® in the refrigerator.*

- Illustrate the third step on a card before reviewing all three steps. Ask him to look at the cards and remember which came first, then next, and then last.

Another idea

On another day, encourage him to make the recipe again so he can use the cards to remember the steps. Invite him to share the cards with a relative so that he can practice explaining the order of events.

Let's read together!

Rabbit Pie
by Penny Ives

Build a Person

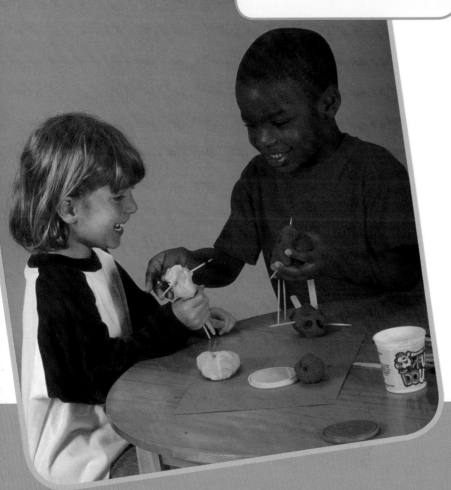

You can use this button for a nose.

Ask questions that will encourage your child to create a detailed person from playdough and craft materials.

Your child will practice using his fine motor skills while thinking about the parts of a whole.

THE
CREATIVE CURRICULUM®
LearningGames®
Copyright 2007 Joseph Sparling

Why this is important

Playing with playdough will increase your child's skills in using his fingers. Building a person helps him remember which parts make up a whole. This game supports your child's fine motor development while increasing his awareness of how the body is put together.

What you do

- Invite your child to make a person with playdough by offering a box of supplies such as popsicle sticks, toothpicks, buttons, and a variety of other small items. **Make sure that younger children do not have access to the small parts that could be a choking hazard.**

- Ask your child, *Which of these could you use to make a person?* If needed, prompt him with questions such as, *What could you use for the legs?*

- Notice how he selects items and attaches them in various ways to make a body.

- Make encouraging comments to your child, but do not participate in the game. Let him choose and create his way: *Those buttons make round black eyes. I see you're using popsicle sticks for legs. What a creative way to make a nose!*

Another idea

Your child could use his imagination to create farm animals, birds, or pets. If he seems reluctant to start, invite a few friends to play with him. The children may get ideas from one another.

Let's read together!

Parts
by Tedd Arnold

I Wonder How She's Feeling

How do you think they felt?

Pause when reading a story to ask your child how she thinks one of the characters in the story feels.

This helps your child become more aware of others' feelings and be able to say a few words about them.

Why this is important

You can guide your child to think and talk about the needs and feelings of characters in stories. Taking an active role in storytime builds early literacy skills and increases her vocabulary. We understand the feelings of others by mentally projecting ourselves into their situation. This skill will help your child begin to be more aware of the feelings and needs of others.

What you do

- Invite your child to read a story with you.

- Pause occasionally as you read to encourage your child to wonder about the feelings or needs of one of the characters. For example, in the story of *The Three Bears*, pause when Goldilocks tastes the bowls of porridge. Say, *I wonder how she's feeling. What do you think?*

- Accept your child's answer and continue with the story. If she needs help answering the question, encourage her to use clues from the illustrations or give her a few choices: *Do you think Goldilocks is full or hungry? You were right. She is full now. She was hungry, so she ate all of the porridge in the little bowl!*

- Limit the number of questions you ask per story, and rephrase any question that seems to be too difficult for your child. You can change *How do you think she's feeling?* to *Do you think she's feeling scared?*

Another idea

Ask your child how she would feel if she were in the character's place. *How would you feel if you lost your favorite toy?*

Let's read together!

Chicken Sunday
by Patricia Polacco

This Is Who I Am

And what does your phone number begin with?

With your child, write and talk about his name, address, and phone number.

Your child will begin to memorize some identifying facts about himself.

Why this is important

Identification data provide a link between children and their adult family members. Playing this game helps your child learn his family name, birth date, address, and telephone number. Especially in case of an emergency, knowing his identifying information gives him a significant form of protection. Seeing this important information about himself in print stimulates his interest in reading and writing.

What you do

- Play word games that help your child remember important personal information. Sing *I am Eva Black. Daddy is Richard Black. Who are you?* Help him answer with his full name.

- Pretend to make a phone call to your house and say your phone number so your child can hear. Repeat it often.

- Talk about your address as you and your child come home: *Here we are at 310 Pine Street.* Ask him questions about his address. *Do you live on Oak Street or Pine Street?*

- Listen as your child repeats the information back to you.

- Show him an identity card such as a driver's license. Point out that it shows your full name, address, and birth date. Talk about how this lets others know who you are.

- Make him a card with his information that he can show to close friends and family members. Put the card in a safe place when you are not playing this game.

Another idea

As your child grasps the information, add more details such as the name of the city where he lives and his zip code.

Let's read together!

Ruby in Her Own Time
by Jonathan Emmett

Add to the Tale

Then new monsters came that were this tall…

After you read a story to your child ask, *What do you think happened next?*

Your child will practice using her imagination to think logically about the future.

THE
CREATIVE CURRICULUM®
Learning Games®
Copyright 2007 Joseph Sparling

Why this is important

By asking your child to talk about what happens after the end of the story, you are helping her establish a new or future idea based on previous events. Your child will have an opportunity to voice an idea about the next logical step in a story. Throughout life we wonder about the future and try to project our ideas into it. Stories, reading, and writing help us do this.

What you do

- Take a minute to reflect on a familiar story after reading it with your child. After *Jack and the Beanstalk*, for example, talk about the fact that Jack now has the treasures and the giant is dead.

- Ask a question that will help her take the story a logical step forward: *What do you think Jack did the next morning?*

- Give her time to think and respond. If her answer does not contain much information, ask questions that may help her elaborate on her idea. Sometimes repeat her words to her so that she knows you are interested: *So he saw the giant again?* She may add more detail to her answer.

- Ask yes-or-no questions if she has trouble continuing the story: *Did he get up? Did he see something out his window?* She may feel more comfortable after you have discussed several stories.

Another idea

Provide crayons, markers, and paper for your child. Encourage her to illustrate what she thinks happened after the story ended. Record her words on her picture.

Let's read together!

Where The Wild Things Are
by Maurice Sendak

Sort Any Way You Like

I like to see how you sort things.

Offer your child colored shapes to sort any way she chooses and ask her to tell you about her groupings.

Your child may begin to see that things can be grouped in many different ways.

THE
CREATIVE CURRICULUM®
Learning Games®
Copyright 2007 Joseph Sparling

Why this is important

Sorting shapes without any direction from you encourages your child to think of many ways to group the shapes. This game gives her experience in considering several possible solutions, which is called divergent thinking. There are no correct answers in this game.

What you do

- Cut two big circles and two little circles from construction paper. Use three colors of construction paper so that you finish with four circles of each color.

- Spread out the 12 circles and say, *We can put these into groups in a lot of ways. Will you show me one way?*

- Observe quietly as your child groups the circles. When she is finished, comment on her work: *You worked very carefully with the circles. Tell me about this group.*

- Mix the shapes again and ask her to find a new way to group them. She will most likely group by color or size, but with practice she may begin to see more ways of grouping.

- Summarize at the end of each round, and talk about the way she chose to put the circles together: *Here are all the large blue circles and these are the little red and blue circles, and here are all the green circles together.*

Ready to move on?

Expand the game by adding multi-colored wrapping paper, more sizes of circles, and other shapes, including 3-D objects.

Let's read together!

Some Things Go Together
by Charlotte Zolotow

Scrambled Stories

Mom put the groceries in the car.

Tell a very short story in the wrong order and invite your child to fix it.

Your child will increase her awareness of why some events must logically occur in a certain order.

Mom bought some groceries.

Why this is important

Asking your child to fix a mixed-up story gives your child practice in mentally arranging stories in logical order. Information does not always reach us in perfect order. For example, in writing a report, information must be gathered from various places and then organized in the most understandable sequence. Practicing organizing information now will help to prepare your child for sequencing complicated information later.

What you do

- Invite your child to listen to a story, but explain that the story might need sorting out: *I've made up some stories to tell. They've gotten a bit mixed up, but I think you can help me straighten them out.*

- Start with a very short story, and explain that it has two parts: *This is one part: In the afternoon Jim came home tired but happy. The other part is: In the morning Jim helped his father paint the house.*

- Ask your child which part of the story should be first and which should be last. Then ask her how she knew which part should be first.

- Move on to longer stories as she successfully practices this skill. A few examples are:

    Two parts: 1. A cat sat on a soft pillow. 2. Soon the cat was fast asleep.

    Three parts: 1. Ed went fishing. 2. Ed fell in the water. 3. Ed sat in the sun to dry off.

    Four parts: 1. Mary woke up. 2. Mary got dressed and ate breakfast. 3. Mary rode on the school bus. 4. Mary said "Good Morning" to her teacher.

Another idea

Make pictures illustrating each part of the story. Give them to your child to use in sequencing the story.

Let's read together!

From Caterpillar to Butterfly
by Deborah Heiligman

Which Is Best?

That tower keeps falling.

Let's talk about some ways you could change it.

When your child faces a problem, offer two possible solutions and let him choose the best option.

Your child will gain experience in considering alternative paths of action.

Why this is important

Providing your child with two possible solutions to a problem encourages him to think about each one before making a choice. With enough practice, considering alternative actions will eventually become a habit for him. Weighing alternatives is a key step in solving problems. Later your child will be able to link this skill with others to solve problems successfully.

What you do

- Encourage your child to pause when he is dealing with a problem. During the pause, calmly and lovingly explain what is happening. For example, if his tower of blocks keeps falling over, say, *That tower keeps falling. It's made you so unhappy.*

- Talk quietly with your child about problem solving. *There are some things that you could do so that won't happen anymore. Let's talk about a couple of them.*

- Invite your child to consider two options for solving the problem. *You could build the next tower wider and stronger at the bottom, or you could decide to build something else – maybe a long train. Which of these ideas would be best for you?*

- Accept any decision he reaches after thinking about both alternatives. If he suggests a third alternative, congratulate him on his creative thinking.

Another idea

Use this process for helping two children solve a problem. When they argue, calmly sit with them, explain the situation, and suggest two courses of action that they can choose from.

Let's read together!

Talk And Work It Out
by Cheri J. Meiners

Little by Little

> *Let's see how soon you can name this picture.*

Ask your child to name a picture as you slowly uncover it.

Your child will practice creating a whole image of the picture in her mind when only part of the image is visible.

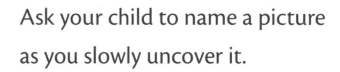

THE CREATIVE CURRICULUM®
LearningGames®

Why this is important

Revealing a picture a little at a time encourages your child to mentally complete the picture. This is called visual closure. Often a person gets only a glimpse of a word or picture, for example, while riding in a car or bus. With good visual closure, a child will be able to read the word or understand the picture even when she can see only part of it.

What you do

- Begin with a familiar book that has large, clear pictures. Choose a book with pictures your child has named before.

- Insert a piece of construction paper so that the first picture is covered when the book is opened.

- Explain, *I'm going to hide some of these pictures from you. But I bet you'll be able to guess what they are. Here's a little peek.*

- Reveal part of the picture by slipping the cover paper part way down. Show as much of the picture as necessary for her to guess successfully.

- Compliment her achievement: *You're right! You named the picture without seeing all of it.*

- Go from page to page in the familiar book before moving on to a book with unfamiliar pictures.

Another idea

Change the game by moving the cover paper in different directions. Sometimes you may uncover from the bottom or side of the picture. You can also use three smaller cover papers and invite your child to remove one paper at a time to guess the picture underneath.

Let's read together!

Seven Blind Mice
by Ed Young

Show Me How It Feels

Can you show me how it feels to be happy?

Talk about feelings and invite your child to show them with his face and body.

The actions of this game will help your child understand, demonstrate, and talk about his own feelings.

Angry?

Surprised?

Why this is important

By calling your child's attention to emotional expressions and by teaching him the names of emotions, you help your child identify his feelings and those of other people. As he learns new ways of expressing his feelings, he will begin to understand that certain ways of showing feelings can help him manage them. He can recognize and express his feelings in a comfortable, accepting atmosphere.

What you do

- Practice expressing feelings with your child while you talk about the names of the feelings.

- Begin with a familiar feeling, for example, *Show me how it feels to be happy*.

- Respond to his actions: *That certainly is a happy dance. It shows me you really feel fine*.

- Show how you look when you feel happy. Talk about times when both of you were happy and reenact the way you showed your happiness.

- Keep the game simple. Talk about each basic feeling as you express it together with facial expressions, other movements, and speech.

Ready to move on?

Play the game another day with various emotions, such as anger, sorrow, excitement, fear, disappointment, annoyance, and so on. Talk about a time when your child felt a particular emotion and about how he and other people show that feeling.

Let's read together!

Yesterday I Had the Blues
by Jeron Ashford Frame

Today I Can

You can snip.

…and thread the needle.

Over a period of days, teach your child a skill that involves several steps.

Your child may notice her own progress. She will see that difficult skills are learned over time.

…and stitch.

Why this is important

This activity lets your child see that she can now do tasks she could not do before. Learning to see her own progress in a series of steps helps your child set and reach realistic goals.

What you do

- Choose a task that can be broken into short, manageable steps. A few examples are: tying shoes, fastening a seatbelt, setting the table, and simple sewing.

- Gather your supplies. For example, for sewing, you need large cloth squares, thread, yarn, sewing needles with large eyes, and scissors.

- Invite your child to sit with you as you help her with the process and the words.

- Show and say each step: *First, I unwind some thread from the spool and cut it with the scissors. I thread it through the needle and knot the two ends together.* Encourage her to repeat the steps.

- Show the next steps: Sticking the needle in and out of the cloth; using all of the thread; cutting the needle loose.

- Help your child finish. Offer positive remarks for each step she does all on her own.

- Clean up together. Discuss what she did by herself. *Do you remember the steps you did by yourself?*

Another idea

Repeat the task at another time. Review the steps: *Can you remember if you threaded the needle? No? Maybe you can practice that today.* Take pictures of your child working, and make a book with her. She can tell you what she did by herself at each step. You can write her words under the pictures.

Let's read together!

Little Bat
by Tania Cox

I'll Get It Myself

I can reach it!

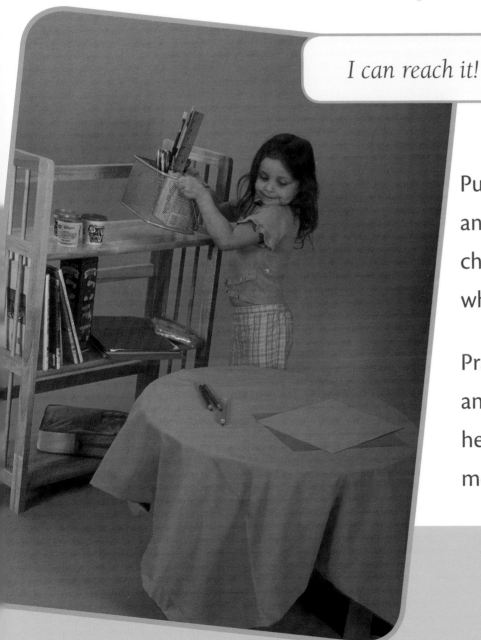

Put a supply of art materials in an easy-to-reach place so your child can create art projects whenever she chooses.

Practice in getting, using, and returning materials will help your child become more responsible.

THE
CREATIVE CURRICULUM®
LearningGames®

Why this is important

Growing up involves increasing levels of independence in many tasks. Although your child may initially come to you with questions, she is learning to work by herself and without interruptions. Independent use of art materials helps prepare her for responsible use of other materials.

What you do

- Begin by planning an art area with your child. A few questions to consider might be:

   Can we create a storage place where she will be able to reach a small stack of paper and boxes of pens, pencils, and crayons?

   During what part of the day may the art area be used freely?

   Is there a trash can nearby?

   Who will help to hang up the finished work?

- Set up the art area with appropriate supplies. Discuss guidelines with your child.

- Make sure you remain available if needed, but otherwise encourage her to work independently.

Another idea

Add art supplies to the art center as your child becomes more responsible with materials. You can include scissors, scrap paper, paste, and paints in addition to crayons and pencils.

Let's read together!

Ish
by Peter H. Reynolds

Mailing a Letter

Uncle Julian will like getting our letter.

Invite your child to participate in sending a letter to a relative or friend.

Your child will think about people who are far away and have a reason for wanting to learn to read and write.

There goes our letter.

THE
CREATIVE CURRICULUM®
Learning Games®
Copyright 2007 Joseph Sparling

Why this is important

Your child can feel connected to his extended family and friends through letter writing. As he practices reading and writing, he also learns the process of sending and receiving mail. Your child will gain a sense of confidence and connection by understanding that his family is larger than the immediate relatives he sees everyday.

What you do

- Use special family times such as birthdays, national, secular, or religious holidays, or personal achievements to help your child become aware of family members who live in other places.

- Help your child send a letter that could include a picture he draws, a photo, or a card you buy together.

- Show him how to put the card in the envelope, and allow him to attach the stamp.

- Talk about the three items that must go on the envelope before mailing: *This is the address where we want the card to be delivered. That's where Aunt Jane lives. This return address tells that you are the person sending the card. The stamp pays for all of the work that it takes to deliver the letter.*

- Explain the next steps in the process as you go together to mail the card. You might take it to the post office or place it in your own mailbox.

- Talk each day about where card might be on its journey.

- Inform the recipient about the activity and ask her if she would please reply to your child.

Another idea

You can also use e-mail with your child as a way to communicate with family at a distance. Talk about the steps involved in sending and receiving e-mail.

Let's read together!

Dear Mr. Blueberry
by Simon James

Double Treasure

Create a treasure hunt for things that have two characteristics, such as being round and being a container.

Your child will need to think carefully in order to classify things in more complex ways.

Why this is important

Your child will practice creating groups that are based on more than one characteristic. Playing this game gives him practice in thinking carefully and systematically about the features of various objects. As people organize information in most everyday situations, it is usually necessary for them to consider more than one aspect of an object.

What you do

- Invite your child to join you on a treasure hunt around the house. For example, say, *Let's look for some double treasures. The things we find must be red, and they must be toys.*

- Check each object he finds by reviewing the characteristics: *This is a toy, and this part is red, so it's a double treasure!*

- Talk about items your child includes but that do not fit the criteria: *That's a fun toy, but it isn't red, so it's not a double treasure. Let's keep looking until we find something that is both red and a toy.*

- At the end of the game, look over all of the objects that he collected.

Ready to move on?

Keep the game interesting by changing the characteristics by which you choose double treasures. You might look for objects that are blue and something to wear, smooth and round, or canned and a vegetable. You can also use a book or magazine to look for pictures of double treasures.

Let's read together!

Round is a Mooncake
by Roseanne Thong

How Do You Walk When...?

Is that the way you walk when you're being very quiet?

Ask your child if he can express some feelings such as tired or rushed in the way he walks.

Your child will use his imagination to express through words and actions his ideas about feelings

THE CREATIVE CURRICULUM®
LearningGames®

Why this is important

When you give your child the opportunity to act out what he imagines, he will learn that exploring his imagination is acceptable behavior. Through imagining we work with, or manipulate, ideas instead of objects. Later, his imagination will carry him beyond his familiar world and allow him to think about places he's never been and solutions to problems that haven't happened yet.

What you do

- Walk in a silly way past your child. When he seems curious, tell him: *I'm walking like I'm dizzy.*

- Invite him to play a walking game. Explain that you will ask him about a new way to walk, and he will answer by walking that way.

- Ask the question the same way each time: *How do you walk when you are*
    - *lost?*
    - *rushed?*
    - *tired?*
    - *very old?*
    - *very young?*
    - *excited?*

- Encourage him to close his eyes, think about how he might feel, and then walk that way.

- Empathize when the task is too difficult. Offer an alternative that he may be more familiar with: *Yes, it is hard to imagine sometimes, isn't it? Can you imagine feeling excited instead?*

Another idea

Invite your child to imagine animals walking in various ways. For example, a lost bird, a tired elephant, an old monkey, etc.

Let's read together!

Glad Monster, Sad Monster
by Anne Miranda

Cut New Lines

You're cutting very carefully.

Draw several types of lines on paper for your child to cut.

His hand and finger skills will increase as he practices using scissors, and your child will feel good about his growing abilities.

Why this is important

Your child can improve his scissor skills in a safe and acceptable way. An available supply of attractive practice sheets can keep him motivated and working to control his cutting. Careful and precise use of the muscles in his hands will be required in many school, work, and life activities.

What you do

- Prepare a series of sheets of paper with lines that help him develop direction in his cutting.

- Make thick lines on thick paper such as construction paper or cut up grocery bags.

- Start with thick, straight lines on the paper. Eventually, make thin straight lines, and then try wavy lines.

- Demonstrate for your child how to cut along the thick, straight line.

- Invite him to practice cutting on whichever lines he feels most comfortable.

- Talk about the shapes he creates and use words such as *straight, curve,* and *corner.*

- Show him how the cut pieces can fit together again: *It fits back together. You made a puzzle!*

- Offer lots of encouragement as he practices.

Ready to move on?

You can continue to challenge him by adding zigzag lines, wavy lines, circles, and more.

Let's read together!

Look! Look! Look!
by Nancy Elizabeth Wallace

Three-Corner Catch

Throw it to me and then I'll throw it to Rohan.

Play an easy game of toss and catch with your child and a playmate.

The children will improve their throwing skills and find that it's fun to take turns and cooperate.

Why this is important

Tossing and catching is a universal children's game in all cultures. Although your child may miss the ball repeatedly at first, he will learn cooperation and turn taking as he practices tossing and catching the ball.

What you do

- Invite your child to join you in a game of catch.

- Toss a large, lightweight ball back and forth with him a few times.

- Suggest an expanded game. *Brett, let's ask Anita if she wants to toss and catch with us.*

- Introduce the new three-person game. *There are three of us. We can play three-corner catch. Each of us will be a corner.*

- Explain the rules: *Brett will throw to Anita, Anita will throw to me, and I will throw to Brett.* You can walk through the motions to help your child understand and remember the order.

- Encourage success during the game by offering encouragement. *Brett, you threw the ball so carefully to Anita. That helped her catch it.*

- Talk about your own actions as well. *I'll step a little closer to you, Brett. It will be easier for you to catch.*

Another idea

Change the game by adding more players, using a different size ball, or increasing the space between children.

Let's read together!

Night Catch
by Brenda Ehrmantraut

I'd Like Help

Will you please help me open this jar?

Teach your child a phrase to make a clear request, such as *Will you please help me with...?* Encourage her to use the phrase when she wants you to assist her.

This teaches your child an age-appropriate method of enlisting help from others.

Why this is important

Your child has already learned to ask for help in very basic ways. Now she is ready to practice using language that enables her clearly to tell what she needs. Knowing when and how to ask for help becomes even more important as your child's tasks become more complex.

What you do

- Choose a phrase that will be easy for your child to use when she needs help, such as, *I need your help with…* or *Will you please help me…?*

- When you need her help, use the statement or question, yourself.

- Anticipate her need and prompt, *Would you like some help? Tell me what you need help with.*

- Be sure to respond each time she attempts to use her new phrase to make a request. Model language for her if she needs help with telling you what she wants.

Ready to move on?

With your child, role-play times when she might ask for assistance. For example, she can pretend to need help with getting dressed, taking a bath, playing a game, or riding a bike.

Let's read together!

Anansi the Spider
by Gerald McDermott

My History in Clothes

You were just 2 when you wore this.

Use clothes your child has outgrown to start a discussion about his past.

Your child will have a chance to think fondly about earlier times and realize how much he has grown and learned.

THE
CREATIVE CURRICULUM®
LearningGames®

Why this is important

Your child's old clothes or toys can serve as memory aids. Together you and your child can talk about his past. Each of us knows we have grown and changed when we compare the present to the past. Since children's early memories aren't usually strong, they need help in recognizing the tremendous growth they are undergoing.

What you do

- Begin by sharing your child's old clothes with him: *Let's look in this suitcase. I've kept some of your clothes in here that you've outgrown.*

- Spread the clothes out and together decide which are from the earliest time and which are more recent.

- Discuss each age the clothes represent: *See how the knees are worn in these overalls? You were crawling when you wore them.*

- Conclude with positive comments about his growth: *You've grown so much. I like the age you are now because we can do so many interesting things.*

Another idea

Use photos, toys, or artwork as another way to talk about his past.

Let's read together!

Joseph Had a Little Overcoat
by Simms Taback

Rules to Grow On

Together make one or two rules that grant your child new privileges and establish a few limits.

By making and following rules, your child will begin to learn that independence is based on responsibility.

After you get your snack, please close the refrigerator door.

Why this is important

Your child can participate in making a few rules that enable her to be more independent. She will begin to think about what everyone needs in order to be independent. As she grows, she will decide on her own personal guidelines, such as how late to stay up before going to bed.

What you do

- Begin by letting your child know that new rules will allow her to do a few tasks on her own.

- Choose a task, such as going outside alone, and talk about what rules would make that option appropriate.

- Ask your child questions that help her think about acting responsibly and safely. For example: Can she tell you before she goes out? Can she play in a space near the house? Can you stay near the window to watch her play? If it is not safe for your child to play outside alone, choose another task, such as answering the telephone. Can she say *hello* and listen to learn who is calling?

- Discuss the possibilities and then establish a rule. It should clearly state the conditions under which the activity can take place.

- Use the rule a few times and then address any problems that arise. Change the rule as needed so that it benefits you and your child.

- Tell her you are proud of her responsible behavior.

Another idea

Many situations can work for this activity such as when and how she can prepare a snack for herself, make her bed when she wakes up, or put her dirty clothes into a laundry hamper.

Let's read together!

Officer Buckle & Gloria
by Peggy Rathmann

Tell How

> *Then you stir and stir.*

Offer your child simple recipe cards so he can tell you or someone in your family how to prepare food.

Your child's confidence will grow as he shows that he can follow the recipe cards and give directions.

Why this is important

Following a recipe gives your child practice with a sequence of directions. Learning to take a more directive and responsible role can lead to new kinds of partnerships. Changing one's role in a familiar situation is a first step for taking on the risk of a new role in a new situation. Studying the pictures and text on cards gives practice in early literacy.

What you do

- Build on the early *LearningGames* activity of making a simple recipe together by letting him direct the action the next time you make it.

- Explain that he will be the one who directs this activity.

- Offer your child the cards that were made for the previous recipe activity.

- Prepare the hot water and then ask for the next step: *Now, what do I do first? What did you and Daddy do first when you made JELL-O®? Do the cards tell you?*

- Help him, if needed, by reviewing the drawings and asking *What do I need to put the JELL-O® in?*

- Ask for each step as you move through the activity. Review all the steps after the recipe is made.

- Talk about how much help he provided: *I'm so happy you're getting big enough to help by telling me what comes next. It's fun to have you as my partner.*

- Try the game again at a later time, and notice how much he can do from memory without relying on the cards.

Let's read together!

A Cake All For Me
by Karen Magnuson Beil

Another idea

Think of other activities that could be carried out using cards, such as making a peanut butter sandwich or folding paper to make a greeting card. Each activity should have no more than three steps until your child becomes skilled at following the directions.

Color and Number Cards

Put red on the number three.

Let your child and a playmate follow directions that contain color and number words and sometimes have more than one step.

Your child will have more experiences with precise directions, like these, in school and in life.

THE
CREATIVE CURRICULUM®
LearningGames®
Copyright 2007 Joseph Sparling

Why this is important

By now, your 4-year-old child recognizes most color words and some number words and probably uses some of them in daily conversation. However, he will need practice to understand these words when they are included in a set of school-like directions. Practice in quickly identifying numbers and letters on paper prepares your child to later learn to read.

What you do

- Invite your child and a friend to play a game with you. Tell the children they will need to listen carefully and remember their colors and numbers.

- Give each child a set of small cards to spread out on the table. Each card should have a color or number printed on it. Start with just three colors and the numbers one through five.

- Ask questions that encourage them to recognize colors and numbers. A few examples are:

    Put your finger on the number two.

    Pick up the red card.

    Put one, two, and three in a row.

    Hand me two colors.

    Can you touch red? Three? Blue? One?

- Offer enthusiastic encouragement during the game: *Good listening! You followed all three parts of that direction!*

Ready to move on?

Change the game by adding more colors and numbers. You can also add letter cards to make the game more challenging.

Let's read together!

A Color of His Own
by Leo Lionni

Let's Imagine

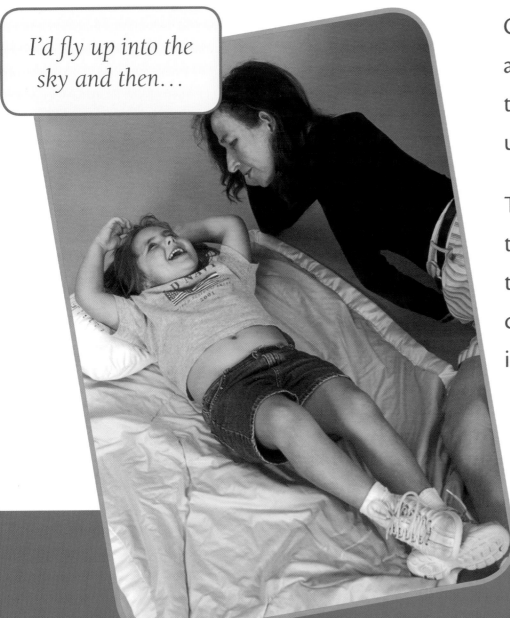

I'd fly up into the sky and then…

Choose quiet times to ask your child questions that encourage her to use her imagination.

This gives your child the opportunity to think creatively by freely choosing and combining ideas in interesting ways.

THE
CREATIVE CURRICULUM®
LearningGames®

Why this is important

Playing this pretend game with your child encourages her to imagine something without any props. Imagining is a way of experiencing something without physical participation. This is a creative way of thinking.

What you do

- Hold your child her on your lap and rock her, or just be close to her as you do during other quiet times.

- Recall a character or situation from a story that you recently read together.

- Ask questions that encourage your child to extend the story, for example, *How did the bear feel when he was on the ice floe? If you had been there, how would you have felt?*

- Offer her an imaginary scenario for her to think about: *If you were going to visit Red Fox, what would you pack in your bag? If you had an invitation to a dinosaur's birthday, what present would you take?*

- Use her experiences to guide your questions. Consider meaningful books, television shows, or recent events that could help her have ideas.

Ready to move on?

Write down her imaginative stories so that you can enjoy them together later.

Let's read together!

Where Do Balloons Go?
by Jamie Lee Curtis

Wondering What Caused It

Look at the new color!

Ask your child questions about the world around him that will lead him to think about why things happen.

As your child begins to link cause and effect, he will think about explanations for changes that he sees.

THE
CREATIVE CURRICULUM®
LearningGames®

Copyright 2007 Joseph Sparling

Why this is important

Your questions can guide your child to think about cause and effect. Asking questions can encourage him to look at ordinary events more closely. The problems we attempt to solve get harder as we grow, but the method of thinking back to what happened before continues to be an effective way to try to understand and solve them.

What you do

- Observe your child's curiosity about events in his day. Almost any daily occurrence can be used for this game. A few examples are water freezing, a broken toy, and leaves falling from the trees.

- Guide him in wondering about cause and effect. Start by saying: *We're going to do some detective work to find out what caused that!*

- Ask questions that help him recount what just happened. *Now let's see. You were painting with two jars of color. What were the colors? Yes, that's right. Red and yellow. Now you have orange paint in the middle. Where do you think it came from?*

- Offer a different idea if his explanation is inaccurate. Do not correct his theory, but simply offer another view.

- Encourage any effort to figure out the cause of the mystery. Your child should feel comfortable exploring all possibilities that he thinks of.

Another idea

Encourage your child to be a detective in discovering what caused something to happen. Give him a notebook, a pencil, and a magnifying glass to use in his investigation.

Let's read together!

White Rabbit's Color Book
by Alan Baker

Clothes for Tomorrow

Which one do you choose for tomorrow?

Offer your child a couple of options in a decision that is coming soon, such as tomorrow's clothes.

Your child will practice considering his options before making a decision.

Red stripes.

Why this is important

Your child will feel more independent when you provide a series of experiences that offer him a choice, such as choosing his own clothes and dressing himself. He can be more independent and successful in many activities if you help him to think and plan ahead before they happen. He will use planning skills later in life while, for example, preparing meals, taking a test, and spending money.

What you do

- Talk with your child before bedtime about an event happening the next day.

- Invite him to choose clothing that will be suitable. Help him lay out the clothes so he can put them on by himself in the morning.

- Guide him to see what options are reasonable so you will not have to veto his choices: *If you're going on a field trip, will you want to wear your comfortable shoes to walk around in?*

- Think with him about alternatives in case of rain or changed weather. Lay out his raincoat and let him decide in the morning if he needs it.

- Make fewer decisions for him as he progresses toward independently choosing and dressing himself.

Another idea

Use this method for other activities that require planning, such as preparing a snack, selecting a book to read tomorrow, or making a gift for someone.

Let's read together!

Ella Sarah Gets Dressed
by Margaret Chodos-Irvine

We Play Relay

You're working together!

Turn an ordinary job, such as bringing toys to the sandbox, into a relay game for your child and a few friends.

By being a member of a fun team, your child may develop a positive attitude about cooperating.

THE
CREATIVE CURRICULUM®
Learning Games®

Copyright 2007 Joseph Sparling

Why this is important

You can provide your child with chances to accomplish tasks cooperatively with other children. Many enjoyable activities, such as team sports, are possible only when groups of people work together. Enjoyable group experiences at age 4 can help your child gain a positive, confident attitude toward later cooperative activities.

What you do

- Create a fun relay game for your child that accomplishes an ordinary task. For example, several children can cooperate in carrying toys to an outdoor sandbox.

- Offer instructions that involve your child and a couple of friends or family members. Assign each child a task in the process of getting the toys to the sandbox. *Let's pretend these sand toys are very big and that you can only carry one at a time. Jeri, you start. Let's pretend that Jeri can only carry a toy from here to the table. Maria will stand at the table to take each toy when Jeri gets it there. Then Gene will carry it to the sandbox.*

- Observe and comment as the children cooperate. *Jeri, it was a good idea to wait for Maria until she got back to the table. Then she was ready for the next toy that you brought.*

- Talk about the game when the children are playing in the sandbox. Help the children remember each child's role.

Ready to move on?

Use a relay game for giving a snack out for a picnic, putting away toys, or moving tricycles to the shed.

Let's read together!

Watermelon Day
by Kathi Appelt

Let's Celebrate

We'll hang the piñata up high.

Prepare for a holiday or exciting event with your child by talking and reading about it in books and then enjoy the special time when it arrives.

Your child's advance knowledge of the holiday will heighten its enjoyment, and he will see that books are one good resource for information.

THE
CREATIVE CURRICULUM®
LearningGames®
Copyright 2007 Joseph Sparling

Why this is important

Your child will learn that useful information can be gained through reading. He can learn about family and culture through celebrating holidays and special events. These special, recurring family rituals give children a way to mark the passage of time and the security of knowing that a familiar event will return.

What you do

- Talk as a family about an upcoming holiday or special event.

- Encourage your child to participate by asking questions and helping with preparation. He may be able to help with food or decorations.

- Explain that not everyone observes this holiday or participates in the event but that it means something special to your family.

- Use books to research the holiday with your child. Learn about how other cultures celebrate the same holidays that you do. For example, you and your child could read about Christmas in Sweden, or Diwali in India.

- Point out to your child how useful books can be for finding information. Use what you find to plan your own celebration.

Another idea

You can research new holidays with your child, too. Answer your child's questions honestly as you both learn about the holiday: *I'm not sure why they make piñatas in Mexico. Let's go to the library and see if we can find out.* Or, *Let's look on the Internet to see why some Japanese families make kites that look like fish.*

Let's read together!

Too Many Tamales
by Gary Soto

Rhyming

Recite a series of rhyming words, and ask your child to say *Stop!* when he hears a word that does not rhyme.

Your child will practice focusing on the sounds that occur at the ends of words.

Lunch…tunch…bunch.

Why this is important

Your child will practice hearing rhyme patterns and eliminating words that do not fit. Recognizing rhymes is another step in understanding how words are put together. Games that help your child focus on the individual sounds of language also help him to develop skills that will be useful in learning to read and spell.

What you do

- Invite your child to play a rhyming game with you. Begin by repeating words he has heard in a nursery rhyme or favorite book such as *Fox in Socks: Fox, socks, box. All those words rhyme. Now I'm going to say more words. But one won't rhyme with the others. When you hear that word tell me to stop. Are you ready? Fox, socks, blocks, clocks, apple.*

- Repeat the words if he does not tell you to stop at *apple*.

- Use nonsense words occasionally to make the game more fun.

- Place the non-rhyming word at different points in the sequence so that your child will not expect it.

Ready to move on?

Invite your child to be the leader and list rhyming words and one that does not rhyme.

Let's read together!

A Was Once An Apple Pie
by Edward Lear

Counting Higher

Use your fingers, objects, or motions to add fun as your child counts to 10 or higher.

Our number system is based on 10, so it is useful to get plenty of practice using these important numbers.

8…9…10

I let him go again.

Why this is important

Counting games offer your child practice using the words from 1 to 10 (or more, if she is ready) in sequence. The numerical system in our country is based on 10. When a child masters 10s, it is a good start on the whole system.

What you do

● Use a fingerplay song to help your child practice numbers from 1 to 10:

Sing	**Play**
One, two, three, four, five,	Close the fingers on one hand to make a fist.
I caught a fish alive.	Enclose your first fist with your second hand.
Six, seven, eight, nine, ten,	Open up the fingers of your second hand.
I let him go again.	Put your hands together and move them back and forth to look like a swimming fish.

● Practice counting with pegs, crayons, or clothespins. You can also use motions such as walking up stairs, hopping on one foot, or clapping your hands to count.

● Say the number clearly as you illustrate it. Encourage your child to say the number during the action.

Ready to move on?

Pay attention to your child's progress with counting. Add more numbers when you think she is ready.

Let's read together!

Feast For 10
by Cathryn Falwell

Think It Through

What's the problem?

When a problem arises, help your child first to name the problem and then to think of two or three possible solutions to try.

With your guidance, your child will learn the basic steps of problem solving.

THE
CREATIVE CURRICULUM®
LearningGames®

Why this is important

Your questions will enable your child to define a problem, identify two possible solutions, and evaluate the alternatives before acting. Simple, systematic problem solving is the foundation for later solving the complex problems of older childhood and adult life.

What you do

● Use these three steps to help your child work through a problem:
  1. Name the problem.
  2. Think of possible solutions.
  3. Choose the best possible solution and try it.

● Focus on everyday situations and guide your child by asking questions that will help him identify and describe the problem. For example, suppose that your child's truck damaged Amy's sandcastle. Prompt: *Amy seems unhappy. I wonder what the problem is.*

● Listen as your child tells you about the problem. Then prompt him again: *It sounds like the sandbox is crowded. What can we do to solve that problem?*

● Give your child enough time to think about solutions. Prompt him with questions only if he needs help. *Do all these activities have to be done in the sandbox?*

● Wait for your child to suggest a few possible solutions before saying, *Which of those ideas do you like best?*

● Encourage your child to try the solution and observe to see whether the problem is solved. If the problem reoccurs, suggest that he try one of his other possible solutions.

Ready to move on?

Talk with your child about a previous problem that could have been solved in more than one way. Talk about what the options were and which option your child chose. This may help him solve a similar problem in the future.

Let's read together!

Tops & Bottoms
by Janet Stevens

Silly Simon

Simon says, "Reach high!"

Play a follow-the-leader game with the rule *Always do what you hear, not what you see.*

This gives your child practice focusing on verbal directions while not being distracted by other information.

Why this is important

Giving conflicting verbal and visual messages gives your child practice in paying attention to the correct direction. The messages we receive are seldom perfectly clear. Sounds or actions often intrude to take attention away from what is most important. Children in school will need to be able to attend to the message from the teacher while other children are talking or other interesting things are happening around them.

What you do

- Invite your child to join you in a new version of the game "Simon Says."

- Explain the new rule: *Always do what you hear, not what you see.* Tell him that sometimes you will say and do the same thing, but at other times you will say one thing and do another. Start slowly and pick up speed as the game progresses

- Make your actions match the words until the third or fourth direction. As you say *Simon says stand on tip-toe,* bend over instead.

- Continue to play, giving directions that contain all the action and space words your child knows: *touch your nose, jump up and down, spin around,* etc.

- Compliment him on his good listening skills when he catches you doing the wrong motion.

Another idea

Encourage your child to be the leader and share the game with friends.

Let's read together!

Ruby the Copycat
by Peggy Rathman

Tricky Directions

Cover all but the third square.

Give directions to your child and some friends to make marks or place color cards on a piece of paper that has been divided into four parts.

Your child will gain experience in following directions working with materials he will use in school, such as paper, cards, and crayons.

THE CREATIVE CURRICULUM®
LearningGames®
Copyright 2007 Joseph Sparling

Why this is important

In this game he will practice listening to directions that can be carried out on paper. A child who knows the word *red* may be temporarily stumped by a complex question that has the simple answer *red*.

What you do

- Use the colored squares from the previous *LearningGames* activity "Color and Number Cards" (#188.) Add a sheet of paper folded into four parts.

- Number the four squares on the folded paper from one to four.

- Give your child a paper and a set of color cards.

- Provide directions that call for actions, and ask questions that call for words. For example:

    Put a color in each square.

    Put colors in the bottom squares only.

    What color is in square number three?

    Where is the color orange?

- Respond with encouragement when your child answers correctly: *I see you chose the red card.*

Another idea

Change the game by using crayons instead of colored cards. Your directions could be *Draw a green circle in the top square*, *Make an X in each of the bottom squares*, and *Turn the circle into a happy face.*

Let's read together!

The Letters Are Lost
by Lisa Campbell Ernst

Same Sounds

Win ... wood.
Same sound!

Say some pairs of words and let your child tell you if their beginning sounds are the same (as in *mouse* and *mat*) or different (as in *tall* and *pan*).

Through repeated playing, your child may begin to pay more attention to the important sounds that come at the beginnings of words.

Why this is important

By playing this game your child will practice focusing on the beginning sounds in words and she may begin using the words *same* and *different* in describing sounds and words. Hearing the beginning sounds of words is an important step in understanding that a word is made up of a series of sounds. The skill of hearing the individual sounds in words will be used later by your child in spelling and reading.

What you do

● Invite your child to join you in a word game. Say, *Listen to these words. Do they sound the same at the beginning? Or do they sound different? Mouse, mat.*

● Repeat the words if your child seems unsure. Exaggerate the beginning sound: *Listen again. Mmmouse, mmmat.*

● Comment positively on your child's successes. *Yes, they are the same beginning sound!*

● Practice with one sound (such as *m*) until you feel your child fully understands the game.

● Add more words to the groupings as you play.

Another idea

Play this game throughout the day such as while riding in the car, taking a walk through the neighborhood, or while waiting in line at the grocery store.

Let's read together!

Polar Bear Night
by Lauren Thompson